Welcome Home

Recipes from Younkers

Welcome Home!

The doors of the first Younkers store opened in 1856, and we've continued the tradition of opening our doors to the communities we serve ever since. At Younkers, we strive to act as a good neighbor, celebrating good times, providing support during difficult times and joining together with our hometowns to make these communities a better place to live, work and play.

For nearly 150 years, Younkers has been your hometown store. Our door has always been open to you, and like a good neighbor, you have visited our store and shared your life with us over the years. And in return, we have a responsibility to be a good and sharing neighbor to you.

We would like to take this opportunity to share some of our favorite recipes with you, our hometown neighbors. You're sure to find just the right tastes inside, whether you're preparing a special dinner, looking for a delicious dessert or you're just interested in trying something new.

Come inside, sample the flavors of the neighborhood—and enjoy! Our doors are always open to you.

Bon Appétit!

This seal assures you that every recipe in this book has been tested in the Better Homes and Gardens® Test Kitchen.

Published by Meredith₆ Books, Publishing Group of Meredith Corporation.
1716 Locust Street, Des Moines, IA 50309-3023

First Edition
ISBN: 0-696-21627-2

Table of Contents

From Our Family to Yours

Younkers Associates share their favorite recipes for brownies, enchiladas, meatloaf and more.

Appetizers & Beverages

These irresistible punches, dips and other nibbles and bites will be a surefire hit at your next gathering.

Main Dishes

Find just what you're craving with this selection of creative entrées for everything from entertaining to everyday.

Vegetables, Salads & Sides

These colorful salads, crowd-pleasing potatoes and other anything-but-ordinary side dishes will add distinction to your meals.

Breads

Experience the aroma and savor the fresh-baked flavor of these terrific muffins, scones and other bakery delights.

Sweets

Indulge friends and family with this selection of irresistible cookies, candies, cakes and desserts.

Pork Tenderloin with Mustard Sauce, page 6

From Our Family to Yours

At Younkers, our Cornerstone
Associates are some of the most
important ingredients in our
recipe for success. These top
performers make it their goal to
do everything possible for their
hometown neighbors. To continue
that tradition, we've invited
several of our Cornerstone
Associates to share their favorite
recipes with you.

Bon Appétit!

Pork Tenderloin with Mustard Sauce

An accomplished cook, Penny Kulp has honed her skills at the Seattle Wine School, Northwest Culinary Academy and the Oriental Cooking School in Bangkok, as well as several other accredited culinary schools. Luckily for us, and for you, Penny also happens to be married to Younkers President and CEO Frank Kulp III. Frank, Penny and the rest of the Younkers family hope you enjoy this favorite from Penny's kitchen. Pictured on page 4.

Prep: 10 minutes   Marinate: 6 to 24 hours   Roast: 35 minutes   Stand: 15 minutes

3	¾-pound pork tenderloins		3	tablespoons soy sauce
½	cup bourbon whiskey			Mustard Sauce (below)
¼	cup packed brown sugar			

1. Place the tenderloins in a large resealable plastic bag set in a large deep bowl. For marinade, combine bourbon whiskey, brown sugar and soy sauce. Pour marinade over meat; seal bag. Marinate in the refrigerator for 6 to 24 hours.

2. Drain tenderloins, reserving marinade. Place the meat on a rack in a shallow roasting pan; pour reserved marinade over meat. Roast the pork in a 425° oven for 35 to 45 minutes or until a thermometer registers 160°F, spooning marinade over meat once. Meanwhile, prepare Mustard Sauce.

3. Cover meat with foil and let stand for 15 minutes before carving. Serve sliced pork with Mustard Sauce. **Makes 12 servings.**

Mustard Sauce: In a small bowl combine ½ cup dairy sour cream, ½ cup mayonnaise, 1½ tablespoons white wine vinegar, 1 tablespoon dry mustard and 1 tablespoon chopped green onion or onion. Cover and let stand at room temperature for 30 minutes. If desired, top with additional green onion before serving. The sauce can be made up to 24 hours in advance and refrigerated. **Makes 1 cup.**

Easy Chicken Divan

Here's a tried-and-true recipe from Karen Detienne, Cornerstone Associate in the Domestics Department in Wausau, Wisconsin. Passed down for generations, this easy oven dish is definitely a family-pleasing favorite.

Prep: 25 minutes   Bake: 25 minutes   Stand: 10 minutes

1   pound broccoli, trimmed and cut into 1-inch pieces (4 cups)
2   cups cubed cooked chicken
1   10¾-ounce can condensed cream of chicken soup
½   cup mayonnaise
¼   cup milk
½   teaspoon lemon juice
¼   teaspoon curry powder
3   ounces American cheese, shredded or torn (¾ cup)
½   cup soft bread crumbs
1   tablespoon butter, melted
    Pimiento strips (optional)

1. In a large saucepan cook broccoli in lightly salted boiling water for 8 to 10 minutes or until crisp-tender. Drain well. Arrange broccoli in a greased 2-quart rectangular baking dish. Arrange chicken over broccoli.

2. In a medium bowl stir together soup, mayonnaise, milk, lemon juice and curry powder; pour over chicken. Sprinkle cheese over sauce. In a small bowl combine bread crumbs and butter; sprinkle over cheese. Bake, uncovered, in a 350° oven for 25 to 30 minutes or until bubbly. Let stand 10 minutes. If desired, garnish with pimiento strips. **Makes 6 servings.**

Pannukakku (Finnish Pancake)

Elma White has been an Associate since 1997 in our Marquette, Michigan store, where she works in the Intimate Apparel Department. She has won the Cornerstone Award every year since its inception! Elma contributed this recipe, which typifies food found in her ancestors' region of Finland.

Prep: 15 minutes   Bake: 25 minutes

¼ cup butter, melted	½ teaspoon salt
5 eggs	Ground nutmeg
1½ cups milk	Warm maple-flavor syrup,
1 cup all-purpose flour	fruit sauce and/or
½ cup sugar	fresh fruit

1. Pour melted butter into a 13×9×2-inch baking pan; set aside. In a large mixing bowl beat the eggs with a whisk or rotary beater. Add milk, flour, sugar and salt; beat until smooth. Pour into prepared pan. Sprinkle with nutmeg.

Bake in a 400° oven about 25 minutes or until puffed and well browned. The pancake will deflate as it stands. Serve with warm syrup, fruit sauce and/or fresh fruit. **Makes 8 servings.**

John's Meat Loaf

You'll find Cornerstone Sales Associate John Gant in the Luggage and Linens Department at our Southern Hills Mall store in Sioux City, Iowa. John says of his recipe, "All of my family loves it. It's easy to make and very tasty." We recommend trying it with the Lemon-Dill Potatoes, page 64.

Prep: 20 minutes Bake: 1¼ hours Stand: 10 minutes

2   eggs, beaten
½   cup soft bread crumbs
½   cup chopped onion
⅓   cup catsup
4   strips bacon, crisp cooked, drained and crumbled (¼ cup)
2   tablespoons spicy brown mustard
1   tablespoon Worcestershire sauce
½   teaspoon salt
2   pounds lean ground beef
Catsup (optional)

1. In a large bowl combine eggs, bread crumbs, onion, catsup, bacon, mustard, Worcestershire sauce and salt. Add meat and mix well.

2. In a shallow baking dish, shape meat mixture into an 8×5×2½-inch loaf.

3. Bake in a 350° oven for 1¼ hours or until internal temperature registers 160°F. Transfer to a platter. If desired, top with additional catsup. Let stand 10 minutes before serving. **Makes 8 servings.**

Napa Cabbage Salad

Cornerstone Associate Jane Klarich manages the Clinique Counter in our Marquette, Michigan store, where she has worked since 1988. She and the other Clinique Associates were named Clinique Counter of the Year in 2000. Jane loves gardening, and if this recipe is any indication, she definitely has a way with vegetables!

Start to Finish: 30 minutes

2	3-ounce packages Oriental noodles with pork flavor
¾	cup sugar
½	cup salad oil
½	cup cider vinegar
2	tablespoons soy sauce
1	head Napa cabbage, shredded (8 cups)
4	green onions, thinly sliced
1	tablespoon olive oil or cooking oil
½	cup slivered almonds
½	cup salted dry roasted shelled sunflower seeds
2	tablespoons sesame seeds

1. Reserve half of the seasoning packet from one package of noodles; discard remaining seasoning. Set noodles aside.

2. For dressing, in a small saucepan combine sugar, the ½ cup oil, the vinegar, soy sauce and reserved seasoning. Cook and stir over medium heat until sugar is dissolved. Remove from heat and cool. Meanwhile, in an extra-large bowl combine cabbage and onions.

3. In a large skillet heat the 1 tablespoon oil. Break up noodles into oil. Add almonds, sunflower seeds and sesame seeds; cook and stir over medium-low heat for 5 to 10 minutes or until lightly browned, stirring often. Add noodle mixture to cabbage mixture. Pour cooled dressing over salad; toss until well mixed. Serve immediately or chill up to 4 hours. **Makes 10 to 12 servings.**

Supper Club Enchiladas

Pauline Hildebrand, a Regional and Divisional Cornerstone winner, works in the Fashion Plus Department at our Merle Hay Mall store in Des Moines, Iowa. This recipe was given to Pauline by her sister-in-law who lives in Texas. "Everyone who has tried these just loves them!" says Pauline.

Prep: 25 minutes Bake: 25 minutes

- 1 **pound ground beef**
- 1 **1.25-ounce package taco seasoning mix**
- 1 **10¾-ounce can condensed cream of chicken soup**
- 1 **8-ounce carton dairy sour cream**
- 1 **4-ounce can diced green chile peppers**
- 8 **7- to 8-inch flour tortillas**
- 1½ **cups shredded cheddar cheese (6 ounces)**
- ½ **cup sliced green onions**
- ½ **cup shredded cheddar cheese (2 ounces)**
  Green onions (optional)

1. In a large skillet cook ground beef until meat is brown; drain off fat. Add taco seasoning mix; cook and stir 2 minutes more. For sauce, in a small saucepan combine soup, sour cream and undrained chile peppers. Cook and stir until bubbly.

2. Spread about 1 tablespoon sauce over each tortilla. Top each with some of the meat, some of the 1½ cups cheese and some of the onions. Roll up and place (seam side down) in a greased 3-quart baking dish. Pour remaining sauce over enchiladas. Cover baking dish with foil.

3. Bake in a 350° oven for 20 minutes or until edges are bubbly. Uncover and sprinkle with the ½ cup cheese. Bake, uncovered, 5 minutes more. If desired garnish with additional green onions. **Makes 4 servings.**

Beef Stroganoff

Brenda Koval, Cornerstone Sales Associate in the Cosmetics Department in Wausau, Wisconsin contributed this recipe. "A very good friend of mine used to make it for me," says Brenda. Thankfully, that friend shared the recipe with Brenda, who shared it with us.

Start to Finish: 30 minutes

1½ pounds boneless beef sirloin steak, cut into bite-size strips
3 tablespoons all-purpose flour
½ teaspoon salt
3 tablespoons cooking oil
3 cups sliced fresh mushrooms (8 ounces)
⅔ cup chopped onion
1 clove garlic, minced

1 cup beef broth
1 tablespoon Worcestershire sauce
1 8-ounce carton dairy sour cream
¼ cup sliced pimiento-stuffed green olives
Hot cooked noodles
Sliced pimiento-stuffed green olives (optional)

1. In a shallow dish or medium bowl toss the steak strips with 2 tablespoons of the flour and the salt. In a large skillet heat 2 tablespoons of the oil. Cook half of the steak strips in hot oil over medium-high heat for 3 to 4 minutes or to desired doneness. Remove from skillet. Add remaining 1 tablespoon oil, remaining steak strips, mushrooms, onion and garlic. Cook, stirring occasionally, for 3 to 4 minutes or until beef is desired doneness. Remove the meat and vegetables from the skillet.

2. Add broth and Worcestershire sauce to the skillet. Stir the remaining 1 tablespoon flour into sour cream; whisk into broth mixture in skillet. Cook and stir until thickened and bubbly. Cook and stir 1 minute more. Add steak strips and vegetables; heat through. Stir in olives. Serve over hot cooked noodles. If desired, garnish with additional sliced olives. **Makes 6 servings.**

Vegetarian Chili in a Crockery Cooker

Sales Manager Fran Triebe, who has worked for the Younkers store in Racine, Wisconsin since 1991, contributed this crowd-pleasing chili. She literally dreamed about this delicious recipe years ago and finally tried it out on the Younkers staff. She's a big fan of Younkers potlucks!

Prep: 15 minutes Cook: 4 hours on high or 8 hours on low

1   30-ounce can chili beans
      with chili gravy
1   15-ounce can black beans,
      rinsed and drained
2   14½-ounce cans diced
      tomatoes, undrained
1   15¼-ounce can whole
      kernel corn, drained
1   cup water
1   cup chopped onion (1 large)
2   cloves garlic, minced

1   teaspoon ground cumin
1   to 2 teaspoons chili powder
1   6½-ounce packet seven
      grain & sesame breakfast
      pilaf
   Shredded cheddar cheese
      (optional)
   Sliced green onions
      (optional)
   Dairy sour cream (optional)

1. In a 3½- or 4-quart crockery cooker combine undrained chili beans, black beans, undrained tomatoes, drained corn, water, onion, garlic, cumin and chili powder.

2. Cover and cook on low-heat setting for 8 to 10 hours or on high-heat setting for 4 to 5 hours. Meanwhile, cook pilaf according to package directions. Stir cooked pilaf into crockery cooker. Cover and cook 20 minutes more or until heated through. To serve, ladle into soup bowls. If desired, top with shredded cheese, green onions and sour cream. **Makes 10 to 12 servings.**

Cream Cheese Rolls

This recipe comes from Dorothy Coulson, who has been a Cornerstone Associate for 14 years in the Customer Service area of our Moline, Illinois store. Dorothy received the Division and Regional Awards for Sales Support for 2001. A great thing about this recipe, she notes, is that the rolls can be made ahead and frozen for serving later.

Prep: 30 minutes Chill: 4 hours

2 8-ounce packages cream cheese, softened
1½ cups shredded sharp cheddar cheese (6 ounces)
½ cup crumbled blue cheese
½ cup butter or margarine, softened
½ teaspoon garlic salt
1 tablespoon half-and-half
1½ teaspoons onion juice*
1 cup finely chopped toasted nuts**
⅓ cup snipped fresh parsley
Assorted crackers

1. In a large mixing bowl beat cream cheese, cheddar cheese, blue cheese, butter, garlic salt, half-and-half and onion juice with an electric mixer on medium speed until well combined. Cover and chill for 4 to 24 hours.

2. Shape mixture into two 8-inch-long, 2-inch-wide rolls. Combine chopped nuts and parsley on waxed paper. Coat rolls with nut mixture. Serve with assorted crackers. **Makes two 8-inch logs (24 to 32 2-tablespoon servings).**

*Note: Look for onion juice in the spice aisle of the supermarket. If it's unavailable, substitute ¼ teaspoon onion powder for the onion juice.

**Note: Toasting nuts or seeds really heightens their flavor. To toast, spread nuts or seeds in a single layer in a shallow baking pan. Bake in a 350° oven for 5 to 10 minutes or until light golden brown, watching carefully and stirring once or twice so the nuts or seeds do not burn. Cool before using.

To make ahead: Prepare as above, except do not roll in nuts and parsley. Wrap cheese rolls in moisture- and vapor-proof plastic wrap. Freeze for up to 1 month. To serve, thaw the cheese rolls in the refrigerator overnight. Roll in nuts and parsley. Let stand at room temperature 30 minutes before serving.

Cranberry Cake with Golden Sauce

LuAnn Hilmer, Administrative Assistant at Younkers Fox River Mall in Appleton, Wisconsin shares this recipe. It's her husband Dean's favorite cake—she makes it for him on his birthday every year. The recipe was given to her by Dean's mother. Now that's a family favorite!

Prep: 15 minutes   Bake: 40 minutes

2	cups all-purpose flour	2	cups cranberries
1	cup sugar	1	cup sugar
2	teaspoons baking powder	1	5-ounce can (⅔ cup)
¼	teaspoon salt		evaporated milk
1	cup milk	4	tablespoons butter
1	egg, slightly beaten		

1. Lightly grease and flour a 2-quart square baking dish; set aside. In a medium bowl stir together flour, the 1 cup sugar, the baking powder and salt. Add milk and egg; stir until just combined. Stir in cranberries. Pour batter into prepared pan. Bake in a 350° oven about 40 minutes or until lightly browned and toothpick inserted in center comes out clean. Cool slightly in pan on a wire rack.

2. For sauce, in a small saucepan stir together the remaining 1 cup sugar, the evaporated milk and butter. Cook and stir until mixture comes to boiling; remove from heat and cool slightly. Serve cake warm in small dessert bowls; spoon sauce over cake. **Makes 9 servings.**

Buttermilk Brownies

Shirley Miller, who has been a Cornerstone Associate for 3 years and was a regional winner for Cornerstone recognition this year, has been with Younkers in West Burlington, Iowa for 7 years. She works in the Children's Department. Shirley loves kids! No doubt kids love her too—especially when she bakes these yummy brownies.

Prep: 20 minutes   Bake: 25 minutes

2   cups granulated sugar
2   cups all-purpose flour
¼   cup unsweetened cocoa powder
1   teaspoon baking soda
½   teaspoon salt
1   cup butter, melted
1   cup water
½   cup buttermilk

2   eggs, lightly beaten
1   teaspoon vanilla
¼   cup butter
2   tablespoons unsweetened cocoa powder
1   teaspoon vanilla
2   cups sifted powdered sugar
     Milk (about 2 tablespoons)

1. Lightly grease a 15×10×1-inch baking pan; set aside. In a large bowl stir together the granulated sugar, flour, ¼ cup cocoa powder, baking soda and salt; set aside.

2. In a medium bowl stir together the melted butter, water, buttermilk, eggs and 1 teaspoon vanilla. Add to flour mixture; stir until smooth.

3. Pour batter into prepared pan. Bake in a 350° oven about 25 minutes or until a toothpick inserted near the center comes out clean. Remove to a wire rack.

4. For frosting, in a small saucepan melt the ¼ cup butter over low heat. Remove from heat. Stir in the 2 tablespoons cocoa powder and the 1 teaspoon vanilla. Stir in powdered sugar and enough milk to make frosting smooth and spreadable.

5. Spoon the frosting over the warm brownies; spread evenly. Cool brownies completely. **Makes 24 servings.**

Honey Party P.
page 32

Appetizers & Beverages

Name your pleasure—
perhaps an
old-fashioned honey-sweet
punch? How about an
all-new take on cocktail
meatballs? Here's an array
of festive ways to kick off
any style of party!

Chilled Artichokes with Two Dips

There's nothing difficult about serving fresh artichokes—these can even be made ahead. For a fanciful presentation, spoon the dips into halved sweet peppers.

Prep: 20 minutes Cook: 20 minutes

4 large artichokes	Assorted crackers
1 lemon	1 recipe Curry Dip (below)
Lemon juice	1 recipe Dilly Crab Dip (below)

1. Rinse artichokes under cold running water, flushing out any dirt between the leaves. Pull off and discard lower petals. Trim stems to 1 inch or less. Cut off the top quarter or third of artichokes. Trim the leaf tips, if desired. Immediately rub the cut surfaces with a piece of lemon; drop the artichokes into a bowl of water with 1 or 2 tablespoons lemon juice added to help prevent browning.

2. In a large stainless steel, nonstick or enamel-coated saucepan cook artichokes, covered, in a large amount of boiling salted water for 20 to 30 minutes or until a leaf pulls out easily. Invert artichokes to drain.

3. Cover and chill artichokes thoroughly. To serve, pull off all outer leaves and arrange on a serving platter with crackers, Curry Dip and Dilly Crab Dip. Discard sharp inner artichoke leaves and fuzzy choke. Slice artichoke heart (the bottom) and add to platter or reserve for another use. **Makes 10 to 12 servings.**

Curry Dip: In a small mixing bowl stir together one 8-ounce container plain yogurt, $\frac{1}{2}$ cup mayonnaise, 1 tablespoon lemon juice, 1 to 2 teaspoons curry powder, 2 teaspoons prepared horseradish and 2 teaspoons grated onion. Cover and refrigerate for 2 to 24 hours. If desired, garnish dip with green onion. **Makes about 1$\frac{1}{2}$ cups.**

Dilly Crab Dip: In a small mixing bowl stir together $\frac{1}{2}$ cup mayonnaise; $\frac{1}{2}$ cup dairy sour cream; 1 cup flaked, cooked crabmeat (cartilage removed); 2 teaspoons finely chopped onion; 1 teaspoon dried dill; $\frac{1}{2}$ teaspoon finely shredded lime peel; 1 teaspoon lime juice and a dash bottled hot pepper sauce. Season to taste with salt and pepper. Cover and refrigerate 2 to 24 hours. Just before serving, if desired, sprinkle with additional crabmeat. **Makes about 1$\frac{1}{2}$ cups.**

Blue Cheese-Walnut Dip

*What makes this tantalizing dip unlike any other is its base—a creamy
yogurt cheese that you make simply by straining plain yogurt.*

Prep: 10 minutes   Chill: 24 hours

4   cups plain fat-free or low-fat
     yogurt*
1   cup chopped walnuts, toasted
     (see note, page 17)

⅔   cup crumbled blue cheese
     Assorted vegetable dippers
        and/or assorted crackers

1. For yogurt cheese, line a yogurt
strainer, sieve or small colander with
3 layers of 100-percent-cotton
cheesecloth or a clean paper coffee
filter. Suspend strainer over a bowl.
Spoon yogurt into strainer. Cover with
plastic wrap. Refrigerate at least
24 hours and up to 48 hours. Discard
liquid in bowl.

2. Transfer strained yogurt cheese
to a medium bowl. Stir in nuts and
blue cheese. Serve with assorted
vegetable dippers and/or crackers.
Makes 2⅔ cups (10 to 12 servings).

*Note: Use yogurt that contains no
gums, gelatin or fillers. These
ingredients may prevent the curd and
whey from separating to make cheese.

Chile Con Queso Dip

This creamy, always-popular melted cheese dip can be whipped up in no time, thanks to the microwave.

Prep: 5 minutes Cook: 5 minutes

1 16-ounce jar salsa (1¾ cups)
16 ounces shredded American cheese (4 cups)

1 tablespoon snipped fresh cilantro
Tortilla chips
Milk (optional)

1. Place salsa in a medium microwave-safe bowl; cover with vented plastic wrap. Cook on 100-percent power (high) for 3 minutes or until salsa is very hot, stirring once.

2. Stir in the cheese. Cover with vented plastic wrap and microwave on high for 2 to 3 minutes more or until cheese is melted, stirring after every minute. Stir in the cilantro. Serve with tortilla chips.

(If mixture becomes too thick upon standing, stir in a small amount of warmed milk.) Makes about 3⅓ cups (12 to 16 servings).

Saucepan method: In a medium saucepan heat salsa until very hot. Reduce heat to low. Gradually add cheese, stirring until cheese is melted and mixture is smooth. Stir in cilantro and serve as above.

Date-Sausage Bites

These bite-size treats are sweet and savory, chewy and flaky—with a little peppery bite. Talk about a unique and irresistible appetizer!

Stand: 20 minutes   Prep: 20 minutes   Bake: 20 minutes

½ of a 17.3-ounce package
frozen puff pastry
(1 sheet)
6 ounces uncooked maple-
flavor pork sausage
½ cup chopped pitted dates
½ teaspoon garlic powder

¼ teaspoon dried sage or
oregano, crushed
⅛ teaspoon crushed red
pepper
⅛ teaspoon ground black
pepper

1. Let puff pastry stand at room temperature for 20 to 30 minutes or just until thawed. Carefully unfold pastry. Cut along folds, making 3 rectangles; set aside.

2. For filling, in a medium bowl combine sausage, dates, garlic powder, sage, red pepper and black pepper. Spread about ¼ cup filling lengthwise down half of each pastry rectangle to within ½ inch of one long edge. Fold the other long side of pastry over meat mixture; pinch edges to seal. Cut filled pastries into 1-inch pieces.

3. Place the pieces on an ungreased 15×10×1-inch baking pan. Bake in a 400° oven for 20 minutes or until golden brown. Serve warm. **Makes about 27 pieces.**

To make ahead: Fill the pastry as directed, except do not cut into pieces. Cover; chill for up to 2 hours. Slice and bake as directed.

Sesame-Soy Meatballs

Ever notice how cocktail meatballs are among the first to vanish from appetizer buffets? These fragrant, Asian-inspired gems are no exception.

Prep: 30 minutes Chill: 1 hour Grill or Broil: 10 minutes

1	pound lean ground beef
⅓	cup finely chopped green onions
¼	cup finely chopped onion
3	tablespoons soy sauce
2	tablespoons sesame seeds, toasted (see note, page 17)

1	tablespoon sugar
20	6-inch wooden skewers
½	of a medium cored, peeled pineapple, cut into 1-inch pieces (optional)
1	medium papaya, peeled, seeded and cut into 1-inch pieces (optional)

1. Mix ground beef, green onions, onion, soy sauce, sesame seeds and sugar in a medium bowl. Shape meat mixture into 40 meatballs, about 1 inch in diameter. Transfer meatballs to a 15×10×1-inch baking pan; cover and refrigerate 1 hour.

2. Meanwhile, soak skewers in water in a shallow bowl for 1 hour; drain. Thread 2 meatballs on each skewer. Grill skewers on the rack of an uncovered grill directly over medium coals for 10 to 12 minutes or until meat is no longer pink, turning occasionally. (For a gas grill, preheat grill. Reduce heat to medium. Place skewers on grill rack over heat. Cover and grill as above.) Or place skewers on the unheated rack of a broiler pan. Broil 3 to 4 inches from the heat for 10 to 12 minutes, turning occasionally. If desired, add a piece of pineapple and papaya to each skewer before serving. **Makes 20 servings.**

Lemon-Basil Cheese Ball

Mix and shape this cheese ball in advance. Just before guests arrive, unmold it onto a serving plate.

Prep: 15 minutes   Chill: 3 hours

1 8-ounce carton mascarpone cheese
1 cup shredded Gruyère cheese (4 ounces)
3 tablespoons finely chopped pistachio nuts
2 tablespoons finely snipped fresh basil
4 teaspoons finely shredded lemon peel
⅛ teaspoon black pepper
Assorted crackers

1. In a large mixing bowl beat mascarpone with an electric mixer on medium to high speed for 30 seconds. Stir in Gruyère. Stir in pistachios, basil, lemon peel and pepper.

2. Line a 2-cup bowl with plastic wrap. Transfer cheese mixture to bowl; cover and chill for 3 hours or until firm. (Cheese mixture can be refrigerated up to 3 days.) Unmold onto a serving plate; remove plastic wrap. Serve with assorted crackers. **Makes 24 servings.**

Honey-Cardamom Crunch

You may think you've seen this snack mix before—but just try it! Cranberries, coconut, almonds and a hint of cardamom make it unlike any you've ever tasted. Consider packing it in decorative boxes or bags for gift-giving.

Prep: 15 minutes   Bake: 40 minutes

⅓ cup packed brown sugar	2 cups tiny pretzel twists
¼ cup butter	1 cup unblanched whole almonds
¼ cup honey	1 cup shredded coconut
½ to 1 teaspoon ground cardamom or ¼ teaspoon ground allspice	1 cup dried cranberries or snipped dried pineapple
6 cups bite-size rice-square cereal	

1. In a small saucepan heat and stir brown sugar, butter, honey and cardamom until butter melts. In a large roasting pan combine rice-square cereal, pretzels, almonds and coconut. Drizzle brown sugar mixture over cereal mixture; toss to coat.

2. Bake in a 300° oven for 40 minutes; stir every 10 minutes. Stir in cranberries. Spread mix on foil; cool. Store in an airtight container. **Makes 13 cups.**

Honey Party Punch

Everyone needs a winning recipe for an all-occasion nonalcoholic punch.
This one will taste great in any season, for any occasion. Pictured on page 20.

Prep: 15 minutes Chill: 4 hours

¼ cup honey
¼ cup boiling water
3 cups water
3 cups unsweetened pineapple
     juice
¾ cup orange juice

¼ cup lemon juice
¼ cup lightly packed fresh
     mint leaves
1 1-liter bottle ginger ale,
     chilled
    Ice Ring (below)

1. In a large bowl combine honey and the ¼ cup boiling water. Stir in the 3 cups water, the pineapple juice, orange juice, lemon juice and mint. Cover; chill at least 4 hours.

2. Discard mint leaves before serving. Pour punch into punch bowl; stir in ginger ale. Carefully slide Ice Ring into punch bowl. If desired, garnish each serving with fruit on a decorative pick. **Makes 12 servings.**

Ice Ring: Pour about ½-inch water into a 3-cup ring mold. Arrange maraschino cherries, halved orange slices, halved lemon slices and fresh mint leaves on top; freeze until solid. Carefully add water to fill mold; freeze again until solid. To unmold, wrap ring mold in a hot towel; invert onto a plate and remove mold.

Colonial Wassail Bowl

There's nothing like a colorful punch to get a party started on the right note. This sophisticated sweet-tart sipper will do the trick. Be sure to use a wine that you like, because its flavor will permeate the punch.

Prep: 5 minutes Cook: 10 minutes

1   750-milliliter bottle dry red wine (such as Burgundy)
2   cups cranberry juice
1   cup sugar
½   cup water
¼   cup lemon juice
6   inches stick cinnamon
¼   cup brandy (optional)
     Lemon slices (optional)

1. In a large saucepan combine wine, cranberry juice, sugar, water, lemon juice and stick cinnamon. Heat just until bubbly around edges; reduce heat. Simmer, uncovered, for 10 minutes. Remove cinnamon with a slotted spoon.

If desired, stir in brandy. Carefully pour punch into a heatproof punch bowl. If desired, garnish with lemon slices. Ladle into heatproof cups. **Makes 12 to 14 servings.**

*Roasted Capon with
Mushroom Stuffing, page 48*

Main Dishes

Whether you're looking for the perfect entrée for an easygoing family dinner or something spectacular for a pull-out-all-the-stops celebration, you're headed in the right direction!

Peppered Chutney Roast

When the occasion calls for a splurge, beef tenderloin is a top choice.
This simple preparation does the rich meat delicious justice.

Prep: 20 minutes Marinate: 4 to 8 hours Roast: 35 minutes Stand: 15 minutes

¾   cup unsweetened pineapple
    juice
½   cup steak sauce
⅓   cup port
⅓   cup Worcestershire sauce
¼   cup lemon juice
1   teaspoon seasoned salt
1   teaspoon lemon-pepper
    seasoning

1   teaspoon dry mustard
1   teaspoon black pepper
1   2½- to 3-pound beef
    tenderloin
1   teaspoon cracked black
    pepper
3   slices bacon, cooked and
    drained
½   cup chutney, snipped

1. For marinade, in a medium bowl combine pineapple juice, steak sauce, port, Worcestershire sauce, lemon juice, seasoned salt, lemon-pepper seasoning, dry mustard and the 1 teaspoon black pepper; set aside.

2. Score meat by making shallow cuts at 1-inch intervals diagonally across tenderloin in a diamond pattern. Repeat on second side. Place meat in a large resealable plastic bag set in a large deep bowl. Pour marinade over meat; seal bag. Refrigerate for 4 to 8 hours (but no longer), turning meat occasionally. Drain, reserving the marinade.

3. Rub beef tenderloin with cracked pepper. Place meat on a rack in a shallow roasting pan. Insert a meat thermometer into the center of the meat. Roast, uncovered, in a 425° oven for 30 to 45 minutes or until meat thermometer registers 135°F.

4. Remove roast from the oven and arrange bacon strips on the top. Spoon chutney evenly over tenderloin. Return the roast to the oven for 5 to 10 minutes more or until the meat reaches 140°F (center will be medium-rare; for a medium to medium-well roast, cook until meat thermometer registers 150°F). The meat temperature will rise 5°F upon standing. Transfer meat to a serving platter. Let stand, covered, about 15 minutes before slicing. **Makes 12 servings.**

Maple-Glazed Pot Roast

Looking for something different for the Sunday roast? This is it! Autumn flavors star in this warming one-dish winner.

Prep: 30 minutes Cook: 1¾ hours

1   2½- to 3-pound beef chuck pot roast
1   tablespoon cooking oil
5   medium carrots and/or parsnips, cut into 3-inch pieces
2   small onions, cut into wedges
2   stalks celery, bias-sliced into 2-inch pieces
½   cup maple syrup or maple-flavor syrup
1   teaspoon finely shredded orange peel

½   cup orange juice
2   tablespoons white wine vinegar
1   tablespoon Worcestershire sauce
1   bay leaf
½   teaspoon salt
¼   teaspoon black pepper
1   medium (about 1 pound) butternut squash, peeled, seeded and cut into 2-inch pieces
¼   cup water
2   tablespoons cornstarch

1. Trim fat from roast. In a 4-quart Dutch oven brown roast on all sides in hot oil; drain fat. Add carrots and/or parsnips, onions and celery to Dutch oven. In a small mixing bowl combine maple syrup, orange peel, orange juice, white wine vinegar, Worcestershire sauce, bay leaf, salt and pepper. Pour over roast and vegetables. Bring to boiling; reduce heat. Simmer, covered, for 1¼ hours.

2. Add squash to Dutch oven. Simmer, covered, for 30 minutes more or until roast and vegetables are tender. Transfer roast and vegetables to a warm platter, reserving pan juices; discard bay leaf. Cover roast and vegetables with foil.

3. For gravy, transfer pan juices to a 2-cup glass measure. Skim fat from juices. Measure 1¾ cups reserved pan juices. (If necessary, add water to equal 1¾ cups.) Return juices to pan. In a small bowl combine water and the cornstarch; stir into juices in pan. Cook and stir until thickened and bubbly. Cook and stir for 2 minutes more. Serve gravy with roast and vegetables. **Makes 8 servings.**

Basil Beef Stew

Soup mix shaves time off preparation, while snipped basil brings a windfall of fresh flavor to the stew. Convenience from the soup mix and freshness from the herb—now that's the best of both worlds!

Prep: 20 minutes Cook: 1½ hours

1 2-pound boneless beef chuck roast	1½ cups packaged, peeled baby carrots
¼ cup all-purpose flour	1 2.4-ounce envelope tomato-basil soup mix
½ teaspoon seasoned salt	2 cups water
2 tablespoons butter	1 large tomato, chopped
1 pound tiny new potatoes, quartered	2 tablespoons snipped fresh basil
2 cups fresh mushrooms, halved	

1. Trim fat from beef. Cut beef into 1½-inch pieces. Place flour and seasoned salt in a plastic bag. Add beef pieces, a few at a time, shaking to coat. In a 4-quart Dutch oven melt butter over medium-high heat. Brown beef, half at a time, in hot butter. Drain fat. Return all of the meat to Dutch oven.

2. Add potatoes, mushrooms and carrots. Sprinkle with soup mix; stir in water. Bring to boiling; reduce heat. Cover and simmer for 1½ hours or until meat and vegetables are tender. Stir in tomato and basil; heat through. **Makes 6 to 8 servings.**

To make ahead: Prepare stew, simmering until meat, potatoes and carrots are tender. Do not add tomato and basil. Transfer to a bowl. Cool quickly; cover and chill for up to 24 hours. To serve, return to Dutch oven and bring to boiling, stirring occasionally. Stir in the tomato and the basil; heat through.

Citrus Corned Beef Sandwiches

Go ahead—pick up the phone! Invite friends to go shopping (or to a movie matinee or an afternoon game), then head home to these ready-to-serve sandwiches fresh from the crockery cooker. Serve alongside purchased coleslaw and Raspberry-Citrus Bars, page 92.

Prep: 30 minutes Cook: 4 hours on high or 8 hours on low Broil: 2 minutes

1   2- to 3-pound corned beef
    brisket with spice packet
1   cup water
¼   cup Dijon-style mustard
¼   teaspoon finely shredded
    orange peel
⅓   cup orange juice
4   teaspoons all-purpose flour
8   kaiser rolls, split
6   ounces Muenster cheese,
    sliced

1. Trim fat from meat. Rub brisket with spices from spice packet. If necessary, cut brisket to fit into a 3½-, 4- or 5-quart electric crockery cooker. Place brisket in cooker. Combine water and mustard; pour over meat.

2. Cover and cook on low-heat setting for 8 to 10 hours or on high-heat setting for 4 to 5 hours. Remove meat; cover to keep warm. Skim fat from juices. Reserve juices; discard whole spices.

3. In a small saucepan stir together orange peel, orange juice and flour; gradually stir in ¼ cup of the reserved cooking juices. Cook and stir until thickened and bubbly. Cook and stir 1 minute more.

4. To serve, thinly slice meat across the grain. Arrange rolls, cut side up, on the unheated rack of a broiler pan. Broil 4 to 5 inches from heat for 1 to 2 minutes or until toasted. Remove rolls from broiler pan. Place meat on roll bottoms. Drizzle about 1 tablespoon cooking juices over meat. Top with cheese. Broil 1 to 2 minutes more or until cheese melts. Add roll tops. **Makes 8 servings.**

Garlic-Thyme Pork Chops

Why not try a rice pilaf mix or a seasoned couscous mix to go with these luscious glazed chops? After all, a super-quick, super-easy weeknight recipe merits an equally simple serve-along. Add some mixed frozen veggies, and dinner is served!

Prep: 10 minutes Broil: 18 minutes

4 pork loin or rib chops, cut 1¼ to 1½ inches thick (about 3 pounds)	3 cloves garlic, minced
3 medium red onions, quartered	3 tablespoons snipped fresh thyme or 1½ teaspoons dried thyme, crushed
1 cup apple juice	½ teaspoon coarsely ground black pepper
1 teaspoon cornstarch	¼ teaspoon salt
1 teaspoon cold water	Fresh thyme sprigs (optional)
1 tablespoon olive oil	

1. On the unheated rack of a broiler pan arrange pork chops and onions. Broil 4 to 5 inches from heat, without turning, for 9 minutes.

2. Meanwhile, for glaze, in a medium saucepan bring apple juice to boiling; boil, uncovered, over high heat for 5 to 6 minutes or until reduced to ½ cup.

3. Meanwhile, in a small bowl combine cornstarch with cold water; stir into apple juice. Cook and stir until slightly thickened and bubbly. Cook and stir for 2 minutes more. Remove from heat. Stir in olive oil, garlic, 2 tablespoons of the fresh thyme or 1 teaspoon of the dried thyme, the pepper and salt. Remove 2 tablespoons of the glaze; set aside.

4. Turn pork chops; broil for 9 to 13 minutes more or until juices run clear. Using a pastry brush, coat the pork chops and onions with glaze during the last 5 minutes of cooking.

5. Remove onions to a small serving bowl. Remove pork chops to a serving platter or dish. Stir the reserved glaze and remaining thyme into onions. Pass with pork chops. If desired, garnish with fresh thyme. **Makes 4 servings.**

Normandy Chicken

Normandy is known for apple cider and Calvados, an apple-infused brandy. Both often make their way into the cooking of the region. Look for hard cider near the beer and wine in your grocery store, or use apple cider or juice.

Start to Finish: 45 minutes

2   tablespoons butter
1   large onion, chopped (1 cup)
½   cup all-purpose flour
8   skinless, boneless chicken thighs (about 1¼ pounds total)
2   medium red tart cooking apples, cored and each cut into 12 wedges

1¼   cups hard cider, apple cider or apple juice
¼   cup dried currants
1   teaspoon dried leaf sage, crushed
½   teaspoon salt
¼   teaspoon black pepper
     Hot cooked rice, potatoes or noodles

1. In an extra-large skillet melt 1 tablespoon of the butter over medium heat; add onion. Cook for 3 to 5 minutes or until tender. Remove onion from skillet; set aside.

2. Place flour in a shallow dish. Lightly coat chicken with flour, shaking off excess. Discard any remaining flour.

3. In the same skillet, melt remaining butter over medium heat. Add chicken. Cook for 4 to 6 minutes or until chicken is brown, turning once. Return onion to pan. Add apple wedges, cider, currants, sage, salt and pepper. Bring to boiling; reduce heat. Cover and simmer about 15 minutes or until chicken is tender and no longer pink (180°F).

4. Serve with hot cooked rice, potatoes or noodles. **Makes 4 servings.**

Turkey with Roasted Garlic Gravy

Prep: 20 minutes Bake: 2¾ hours Stand: 15 minutes

1	8- to 12-pound turkey
2	tablespoons olive oil
1	head garlic
¼	cup all-purpose flour

1	14-ounce can chicken broth
1	tablespoon snipped fresh sage or 1½ teaspoons dried sage, crushed

1. Remove neck and giblets from body and neck cavities of turkey. Rinse the inside of turkey; pat dry with paper towels. Pull neck skin to the back of turkey; fasten with skewers or wooden toothpicks. Tuck the ends of the drumsticks under the band of skin across the tail. If there is no band of skin, tie the drumsticks securely to the tail. Twist wing tips under the back.

2. Place turkey, breast side up, on a rack in a shallow roasting pan. Brush with oil and sprinkle with 1 teaspoon salt and ½ teaspoon pepper. Insert a meat thermometer into the center of one of the inside thigh muscles (do not touch bone). Cover turkey loosely with foil. Roast in a 325° oven for 2¾ to 3 hours.

3. Wrap garlic in foil; place next to turkey in oven. Roast garlic 1 hour or until soft. Remove from oven; set aside.

4. During the last 45 minutes of roasting, remove foil from turkey. Cut band of skin or string between drumsticks so thighs cook evenly. Roast until thermometer registers 180°F. The juices should run clear and drumsticks should move easily in their sockets. Remove turkey from oven. Cover; let stand 15 to 20 minutes before carving.

5. Meanwhile, scrape the drippings and browned bits from roasting pan into a 1-cup glass measure. Let stand 5 minutes or until fat rises to the top. Skim fat. Cut ½ inch off top of roasted garlic and squeeze the pulp from cloves into a small bowl. With a fork, mash the garlic until almost smooth; set aside. In a small bowl stir flour and ¼ cup of the broth until smooth. In a small saucepan combine the reserved drippings, garlic and sage. Bring to boiling over medium heat. Slowly whisk in flour mixture and remaining 1½ cups broth. Cook and stir over medium heat until mixture is thickened and bubbly. Cook and stir 2 minutes more. Remove from heat. Season to taste with additional salt and pepper. If desired, strain gravy mixture through a fine mesh strainer to remove bits of garlic and sage.

6. Carve turkey. Serve with gravy.
Makes 12 to 14 servings.

Linguine with Nuts and Gorgonzola

Here's a rich and opulent dish that's ready in 15 minutes. Serve with vinaigrette-tossed gourmet greens and crusty bread, and treat yourself to something special in nothing flat.

Start to Finish: 15 minutes

1 9-ounce package refrigerated linguine or fettuccine	½ cup crumbled Gorgonzola or blue cheese (2 ounces)
¾ cup chopped hazelnuts (filberts), pecans and/or pine nuts	¼ cup shredded Parmesan cheese (1 ounce)
1 tablespoon butter	2 tablespoons snipped fresh basil
1 tablespoon olive oil	Fresh basil (optional)

1. Cook pasta in boiling water according to package directions; drain. Return to pan; keep warm.

2. Meanwhile, in a medium skillet cook the hazelnuts, pecans and/or pine nuts in butter and olive oil until toasted and butter begins to brown, stirring frequently. Add nut mixture to pasta. Add the Gorgonzola or blue cheese, Parmesan cheese and the snipped basil, tossing gently to coat. Transfer to a serving platter. If desired, garnish with fresh basil. **Makes 4 servings.**

Chicken Osso Buco

This hearty, home-style dish is modeled after a favorite Italian stew that's made with braised veal shanks. Enjoy it on a cold winter night with a crisp green salad and a glass of Chianti.

Prep: 20 minutes Cook: 50 minutes

8 medium chicken drumsticks (about 2 pounds)	1 8-ounce can tomato sauce
2 tablespoons all-purpose flour	¼ cup chicken broth
2 tablespoons olive oil	1 teaspoon finely shredded lemon peel
½ cup chopped carrot	1 tablespoon lemon juice
½ cup chopped onion	1 sprig fresh thyme
½ cup chopped celery	1 bay leaf
4 cloves garlic, minced	2 cups dried penne pasta
½ cup dry white wine or chicken broth	Snipped fresh parsley (optional)

1. Remove skin from chicken. Place flour in a plastic bag. Add chicken, a few pieces at time, shaking to coat. In a 10-inch skillet brown chicken in hot oil over medium heat about 5 minutes per side or until golden. Remove chicken; set aside.

2. Add carrot, onion, celery and garlic to the skillet. Cook and stir for 4 to 5 minutes or until lightly brown. Carefully add wine to skillet, scraping up any brown bits. Stir in tomato sauce, the ¼ cup chicken broth, the lemon peel, lemon juice, thyme and bay leaf.

3. Return chicken to skillet. Bring mixture to boiling; reduce heat. Cover and simmer for 35 to 40 minutes more or until chicken is no longer pink (180°F). Discard thyme and bay leaf. Meanwhile, prepare penne according to package directions. Drain well.

4. To serve, spoon chicken and sauce over pasta. If desired, garnish with fresh parsley. **Makes 4 servings.**

Roasted Capon with Mushroom Stuffing

This is a great dinner choice for a small crowd. Pictured on page 34.

Prep: 30 minutes Roast: 1¾ hours Stand: 10 minutes

- 8 ounces mixed mushrooms (cremini, shiitake, button or portobello), chopped
- ½ cup thinly sliced green onions
- ¼ cup butter or margarine
- 8 cups sage-onion stuffing mix
- ½ cup coarsely chopped walnuts, toasted (see note, page 17)
- ⅔ to 1 cup chicken broth
- 1 5- to 7-pound capon
- 2 tablespoons olive oil
- 2 tablespoons snipped fresh sage
- 1½ teaspoons coarsely ground black pepper
- ¼ cup chicken broth (optional)
- 2 teaspoons olive oil

1. For stuffing, in a medium saucepan cook mushrooms and green onions in butter until tender; remove from heat. Place stuffing mix and nuts in a bowl; add mushroom mixture. Add enough chicken broth to moisten, tossing lightly.

2. Season body cavity of capon with salt. Combine the 2 tablespoons oil, the fresh sage and pepper. Slip your fingers between the skin and breast meat of the bird and between the skin and leg meat, forming pockets. Spoon the sage-oil mixture into pockets, rubbing with your fingers to evenly distribute mixture. Lightly spoon stuffing into body cavity; use no more than ¾ cup stuffing per pound of capon. (Place any remaining stuffing in casserole. Cover; chill. If desired, before baking, add the ¼ cup additional chicken broth to moisten.) Bake stuffing alongside capon for the last 30 to 45 minutes of roasting or until heated through.

3. Tie the drumsticks securely to tail; twist wing tips under back. Place capon, breast side up, on a rack in a shallow roasting pan. Brush with the 2 teaspoons oil. Insert a meat thermometer into the center of one of the inside thigh muscles (do not touch the bone). Roast, uncovered, in a 325° oven for 1¾ to 2½ hours or until meat thermometer registers 180°F to 185°F. Juices should run clear and drumsticks should move easily in their sockets.

4. Remove capon from oven. Cover and let stand 10 minutes before carving. Serve with stuffing. **Makes 8 servings.**

Red Pepper Lasagna

Chefs in France often nestle a white sauce between the layers of their lasagna.
That's the secret to this luscious take on the classic crowd-pleaser.

Prep: 50 minutes Bake: 35 minutes Stand: 20 minutes

2	7-ounce jars roasted red sweet peppers, drained
1	tablespoon olive oil
1	28-ounce can crushed tomatoes, undrained
½	cup snipped fresh basil
4	cloves garlic, minced
¾	teaspoon black pepper
½	teaspoon salt
8	ounces sweet or hot bulk Italian sausage, browned and drained (optional)
⅓	cup butter
⅓	cup all-purpose flour
½	teaspoon ground nutmeg
½	teaspoon salt
3	cups milk
12	no-boil lasagna noodles
1¼	cups finely shredded Parmesan cheese

1. Cut red peppers into thin strips. In a large saucepan cook peppers in hot oil over medium heat 1 minute. Stir in tomatoes, basil, garlic, black pepper and the ½ teaspoon salt. Bring to boiling; reduce heat. Simmer, uncovered, 20 minutes, stirring often. Set aside to cool. If desired, stir in cooked sausage.

2. For white sauce, in a medium saucepan melt butter. Stir in flour, nutmeg and the remaining ½ teaspoon salt until smooth. Add milk all at once. Cook and stir until thickened and bubbly. Set aside to cool.

3. To assemble, grease the bottom of a 3-quart rectangular baking dish. Cover bottom with 3 lasagna noodles. Spread about 1 cup of the red pepper sauce over the pasta. Top with ¾ cup of the white sauce, spreading evenly; sprinkle with about ¼ cup of the cheese. Repeat three more layers with the remaining pasta, red sauce, white sauce and cheese. Be sure to cover top layer of noodles completely with sauce. Sprinkle with remaining cheese.

4. Bake, uncovered, in a 350° oven 35 to 40 minutes or until bubbly and light brown on top. Let lasagna stand 20 minutes before serving. **Makes 8 servings.**

Dilled Salmon with Stir-Fried Vegetables

This colorful dish tastes like something you'd expect to enjoy (and pay top dollar for) at a trendy bistro. It's really surprisingly simple.

Prep: 50 minutes Cook: 20 minutes

1	pound fresh or frozen skinless salmon fillets, cut 1 inch thick
¼	teaspoon salt
¼	cup apple jelly
3	tablespoons rice vinegar or white vinegar
2	tablespoons water
1	tablespoon soy sauce
1	teaspoon cornstarch
½	teaspoon dried dill
1	tablespoon cooking oil
1½	cups carrots, cut into thin strips, or packaged shredded carrots
1½	cups parsnips, turnips, or rutabagas, cut into thin strips
1	small red sweet pepper, seeded and cut into short, thin pieces
4	green onions, thinly sliced lengthwise and cut into 1½-inch strips
	Cracked colored peppercorns

1. Thaw fish, if frozen. Cut into 4 serving-size pieces. Arrange on the greased rack of an unheated broiler pan. Sprinkle with salt. Broil 4 inches from heat for 5 minutes. Using a spatula, carefully turn fish over. Broil 3 to 7 minutes more or until fish flakes easily with a fork.

2. For sauce, in a small bowl stir together jelly, vinegar, water, soy sauce, cornstarch and dill. Set aside.

3. Heat oil in a large skillet or wok over medium-high heat. Add carrots and parsnips to skillet; stir-fry for 5 to 6 minutes until crisp-tender (add more oil as necessary during cooking). Remove and keep warm. Add red pepper and green onions to skillet; stir-fry for 1 to 2 minutes or until crisp-tender. Add to carrots and parsnips. Add the sauce to skillet. Cook and stir until thickened and bubbly. Cook and stir for 2 minutes more.

4. To serve, spoon warm vegetables onto plates. Drizzle with some of the sauce. Top with salmon. Spoon remaining sauce over salmon. Sprinkle with peppercorns. If desired, garnish with fresh dill sprigs. **Makes 4 servings.**

Baked Italian Omelet

When you're having guests for breakfast or brunch, don't fret over fussy omelets. This fix-and-forget egg dish bakes while you mingle.

Prep: 20 minutes Bake: 30 minutes Stand: 10 minutes

1 10-ounce package frozen chopped spinach, thawed
8 eggs, beaten
1 cup ricotta cheese
½ cup milk
½ teaspoon dried basil, crushed
¼ teaspoon salt
¼ teaspoon fennel seeds, crushed

¼ teaspoon black pepper
1 cup chopped tomatoes
1 cup shredded mozzarella cheese (4 ounces)
½ cup thinly sliced green onions
½ cup diced salami or ham
¼ cup finely shredded Parmesan cheese

1. Drain thawed spinach well, pressing out excess liquid; set aside. In a large bowl combine eggs and ricotta cheese; beat just until combined. Stir in milk, basil, salt, fennel seeds and pepper. Stir in spinach, tomatoes, mozzarella, green onions and salami.

2. Pour mixture into a greased 3-quart rectangular baking dish. Sprinkle with Parmesan cheese. Bake in a 325° oven for 30 to 35 minutes or until a knife inserted near center comes out clean. Let stand for 10 minutes. To serve, cut into rectangles. **Makes 6 to 8 servings.**

Salmon and Eggs Benedict

This brunch dish is as impressive as Eggs Benedict—but much, much easier because there are no eggs to poach and the hollandaise starts with a mix.

Prep: 30 minutes Bake: 25 minutes

1   1.25-ounce or 0.9-ounce envelope hollandaise sauce mix (to make about 1¼ cups sauce)
2   tablespoons capers, drained
½   teaspoon finely shredded lemon peel
6   eggs
¼   cup milk
⅛   teaspoon black pepper
2   tablespoons butter or margarine
3   English muffins, split and toasted
6   ounces thinly sliced, smoked salmon (lox-style) or Canadian-style bacon
¾   cup soft bread crumbs

1. Prepare sauce mix according to package directions. Stir in capers and lemon peel. Cover and set aside.

2. Beat together eggs, milk and pepper. In a large skillet melt 1 tablespoon of the butter over medium heat. Pour in egg mixture. Cook without stirring until mixture begins to set on top and around edge. Using a spatula, lift and fold partially cooked eggs so uncooked portion flows underneath. Continue cooking for 3 to 4 minutes or until eggs are set but still moist.

3. Spread about ½ cup of the sauce over bottom of a 2-quart rectangular baking dish. Arrange muffins (cut side up) on top of sauce in dish. Divide salmon or Canadian-style bacon into six equal portions. Place one portion, folding as necessary, on top of each muffin half. Spoon eggs onto muffin stacks, dividing evenly. Spoon remaining sauce over eggs.

4. For crumb topping, melt remaining 1 tablespoon butter. Add bread crumbs, tossing lightly to coat. Sprinkle over muffin stacks. Bake, uncovered, in a 350° oven about 15 minutes or until heated through. **Makes 6 servings.**

To make ahead: Prepare as directed through step 2. Cover; chill the sauce and eggs separately in refrigerator up to 24 hours. Prepare crumb topping. Cover; refrigerate up to 24 hours. To serve, assemble egg stacks as directed in step 3. Sprinkle topping over egg stacks. Bake, covered, in a 350° oven about 25 minutes or until heated through.

Lemon-Dill Potatoes,
page 64

Vegetables, Salads & Sides

*Looking for surefire ways to
round out memorable
menus? Start here with
hearty Make-Ahead
Mashed Potatoes, an
elegant Mesclun Salad with
Roasted Pears and other
side-dish standouts.*

Mesclun Salad with Roasted Pears

*Serve this special salad through the fall and winter months. Roast
pears to intensify their flavor and toss with sherry vinaigrette
and mesclun (an assortment of young, small salad greens).
Select Bosc pears for roasting—they hold their shape best.*

Prep: 15 minutes   Roast: 20 minutes

2 large (1 pound total) Bosc
   pears, peeled, cored and
   sliced ¼ inch thick
1 tablespoon olive oil
¼ teaspoon salt
⅛ teaspoon freshly ground
   black pepper
¼ cup olive oil
2 tablespoons sherry vinegar
   or balsamic vinegar

2 teaspoons finely chopped
   shallots
1 teaspoon honey
¼ teaspoon salt
⅛ teaspoon freshly ground
   black pepper
2 5-ounce bags mesclun salad
   greens or spring salad mix
   (16 cups)
3 ounces blue cheese,
   crumbled

1. Line a 15×10×1-inch baking pan with
foil. Place pear slices in prepared pan.
Drizzle with the 1 tablespoon olive oil.
Sprinkle with the ¼ teaspoon salt and
the ⅛ teaspoon pepper; toss to coat.
Arrange slices in a single layer. Roast
slices, uncovered, in a 425° oven for
20 to 25 minutes or until pears are
golden and edges are crisp and brown,
gently stirring and rearranging once.
Watch closely the last few minutes of
roasting. Cool in pan on a wire rack.

2. In a screw-top jar combine the
¼ cup olive oil, the vinegar, shallots,
honey, the ¼ teaspoon salt and the
⅛ teaspoon pepper. Cover and shake
well to combine.

3. Arrange greens in a large bowl. Add
pear slices and cheese. Drizzle with the
dressing mixture and toss to coat. **Makes
12 servings.**

Broccoli Salad

*Pecans make this simple salad a little richer. Tote it to your next potluck
and you won't have to worry about taking any leftovers home.*

Prep: 30 minutes Chill: 2 hours

6   cups small broccoli florets
    (about 1 pound)*
8   slices bacon, cooked crisp,
    drained and crumbled
1   cup pecan pieces
½   cup raisins

½   medium red onion, chopped
¾   cup mayonnaise or salad
    dressing
2   tablespoons sugar
2   tablespoons red wine vinegar

1. In a large saucepan cook broccoli in a small amount of lightly salted boiling water for 1 minute. Rinse broccoli with cold water and drain; let cool.

2. In a large bowl combine the cooled broccoli, crumbled bacon, pecans, raisins and red onion.

3. In a small bowl stir together mayonnaise, sugar and vinegar until well mixed. Pour the dressing over the broccoli mixture; toss to coat. Cover and chill for 2 to 24 hours. Stir salad before serving. **Makes 8 to 10 servings.**

*Note: You'll need 2 to 3 stalks of broccoli (about 1 pound) to yield the 6 cups of chopped broccoli called for in this recipe. Remove the outer leaves and trim and discard the tough portions of the stems.

Citrus-Sparked Salad

If you find winter salads a little ho-hum, remember this beauty.
It boasts plenty of color and sparkle from grapes, citrus fruit and,
if desired, pomegranate seeds.

Prep: 25 minutes Chill: 30 minutes

⅓ cup salad oil
⅓ cup orange juice
¼ cup balsamic vinegar
4 teaspoons honey
¼ teaspoon cracked black
   pepper
3 medium pink grapefruit
3 medium oranges

1½ cups green and/or red
   seedless grapes, halved if
   desired
3 tablespoons pomegranate
   seeds (optional)
1 head red-tip or green leaf
   lettuce, torn

1. For dressing, in a screw-top jar combine oil, orange juice, vinegar, honey and pepper. Cover and shake well until combined. Refrigerate at least 30 minutes.

2. Use a small sharp knife to peel grapefruit and oranges, removing as much of the white pith as possible. Section fruit and place in a large bowl. Add grapes and, if desired, pomegranate seeds to citrus fruit.

3. To serve, arrange torn lettuce on individual salad plates and top with fruit mixture. (This step may be done up to 1 hour before serving.) Shake dressing and drizzle over salads. **Makes 12 servings.**

To make ahead: Refrigerate dressing for up to 3 days. Section grapefruit and oranges and, if desired, prepare pomegranate seeds; cover and chill for up to 24 hours. Drain fruit before using.

Chestnut Dressing

If you look for intriguing side dishes to make holiday meals extra special, then this stuffing should be part of your repertoire! Roasted chestnuts make it especially festive.

Prep: 50 minutes   Bake: 40 minutes

2   pounds fresh chestnuts in shells or two 10-ounce cans whole, peeled chestnuts packed in water
½   cup chopped celery
½   cup chopped onion
2   tablespoons butter or margarine

2   tablespoons whipping cream, half-and-half, light cream or milk
¾   teaspoon salt
¼   teaspoon dried thyme, crushed
¼   teaspoon black pepper
1   cup soft bread crumbs
    Snipped fresh parsley

1. To shell fresh chestnuts, cut an X on the flat side of each chestnut. Place in a large shallow baking pan. Roast in a 400° oven for 15 minutes, stirring occasionally. Peel chestnuts while still warm.

2. Cook peeled chestnuts in boiling water for 15 minutes or until just tender. Drain and cool slightly. (If using canned chestnuts, place them in a colander; rinse with cool water and drain.)

3. Coarsely chop chestnuts. Place in a large bowl; set aside.

4. In a medium saucepan cook celery and onion in butter until tender. Remove from heat. Stir in cream, salt, thyme and pepper. Add celery mixture and bread crumbs to chestnuts; toss gently to combine.

5. Spoon into a 1½-quart casserole. Cover and bake in a 325° oven for 40 to 45 minutes or until heated through. (Or bake in a 375° oven about 30 minutes or until heated through.) Sprinkle with snipped fresh parsley. **Makes 8 servings.**

Winter Fruit Cup

It's the brown sugar that adds the "Wow!" factor to this creamy-topped fruit cup.
Try it for brunch alongside the Salmon and Eggs Benedict, page 53, or the
Baked Italian Omelet, page 52.

Prep: 30 minutes Chill: 2 hours

4 medium oranges, peeled and sectioned
3 medium apples, cored and chopped (remove peel, if desired)
2 large grapefruit, peeled and sectioned

¼ cup granulated sugar
¼ cup butter
½ cup packed brown sugar
1 8-ounce carton dairy sour cream
1 teaspoon vanilla
   Brown sugar (optional)

1. In a large bowl combine oranges, apples, grapefruit and granulated sugar; toss to mix. Cover and refrigerate for 2 to 4 hours, stirring mixture occasionally.

2. For sauce, in a small saucepan melt butter over medium-low heat. Stir in the ½ cup brown sugar. Cook and stir until sugar dissolves and mixture bubbles. Remove from heat. Gradually stir in sour cream and vanilla. Serve warm sauce over chilled fruit. If desired, sprinkle each serving with additional brown sugar. **Makes 6 servings.**

Green Bean and Sweet Onion Gratin

The ever-popular green bean casserole gets a gourmet update with a creamy white sauce, frozen green beans instead of canned, and fresh sweet onions (try Vidalia, Texas 1015 or Walla Walla).

Prep: 20 minutes Bake: 30 minutes Stand: 10 minutes

1	16-ounce package frozen cut green beans	⅛	teaspoon ground nutmeg
1	pound sweet onions, halved and thinly sliced	1	cup chicken broth
¼	cup butter or margarine	1	cup half-and-half, light cream or milk
¼	cup all-purpose flour	1½	cups soft bread crumbs
½	teaspoon salt	3	tablespoons grated Parmesan cheese
¼	teaspoon black pepper	2	tablespoons olive oil

1. Cook frozen green beans according to package direction. Drain well; set aside.

2. Meanwhile, in a medium saucepan cook onion slices in a small amount of boiling water for 4 to 5 minutes or until tender. Drain; set aside.

3. In the same saucepan melt butter. Stir in flour, salt, pepper and nutmeg. Add broth and half-and-half. Cook and stir until mixture is thickened and bubbly.

4. In an ungreased 2-quart baking dish, layer half of the beans, all of the onions, then the remaining beans. Spoon sauce over all.

5. In a small bowl toss together bread crumbs, cheese and olive oil; sprinkle over vegetables. Bake, uncovered, in a 325° oven for 30 to 35 minutes or until bubbly. Let stand 10 minutes. **Makes 6 servings.**

To make ahead: Prepare as directed, except do not top with the bread crumb mixture. Cover baking dish; chill up to 24 hours. Wrap bread crumb mixture separately; chill. To serve, sprinkle casserole with bread crumb mixture. Bake, uncovered, in a 325° oven for 50 to 55 minutes or until hot.

Lemon-Dill Potatoes

Fresh dill, tangy lemon juice and a hint of garlic help these twice-baked potatoes veer well off the beaten path. Try these with meat loaf, pork roast or oven-baked barbecued chicken. Pictured on page 54.

Prep: 50 minutes   Bake: 20 minutes

4 large baking potatoes	1 tablespoon lemon juice
⅓ cup dairy sour cream	½ teaspoon garlic salt
¼ cup butter or margarine, melted	⅛ teaspoon black pepper
2 tablespoons finely snipped fresh dill or 1½ teaspoons dried dill	Paprika (optional)
	Fresh dill sprigs (optional)
	Lemon wedges (optional)

1. Scrub potatoes thoroughly with a brush. Pat dry with paper towels. Prick potatoes with a fork. Bake in a 425° oven for 40 to 60 minutes or until tender.

2. Cut potatoes in half lengthwise. Gently scoop pulp out of each potato half, leaving a thin shell. Place potato pulp in a large mixing bowl. Add sour cream, 3 tablespoons of the butter, the snipped fresh dill or dried dill, lemon juice, garlic salt and pepper to the potatoes. Beat with an electric mixer on low speed until smooth. Mound the mixture into the potato shells.

3. Place in a 3-quart rectangular baking dish. Brush potatoes with remaining butter. If desired, sprinkle with paprika. Bake in a 425° oven about 20 minutes or until lightly brown. If desired, garnish with dill sprigs and lemon wedges. **Makes 8 servings.**

Make-Ahead Mashed Potatoes

Forget last-minute mashing and gravy making! These mashed potatoes are definitely in the do-ahead category, and so rich you can forgo the gravy.

Prep: 50 minutes Chill: 6 hours Bake: 1 hour 20 minutes

5 pounds baking potatoes	½ teaspoon garlic powder
1 8-ounce package cream cheese, softened	¼ teaspoon black pepper
1 8-ounce carton dairy sour cream	2 tablespoons butter or margarine, cut up
1 teaspoon salt	Paprika
1 teaspoon dried parsley	

1. Peel and quarter potatoes. In a large saucepan cook potatoes, covered, in a moderate amount of boiling water for 20 to 25 minutes or until tender. Drain and mash.

2. Add cream cheese to hot mashed potatoes and stir until combined. Stir in sour cream, salt, parsley, garlic powder and pepper. Spread mashed potatoes in a 3-quart lightly greased casserole. Dot with butter; sprinkle with paprika. Cover and chill in refrigerator for at least 6 hours or up to 24 hours.

3. To serve, bake, covered, in a 350° oven about 1 hour and 20 minutes or until an instant-read thermometer inserted in center registers 165°F. Makes 12 servings.

Cheesy Wild Rice Casserole

So creamy, so good and so easy! Serve this alongside a Sunday roast or a holiday ham—and take advantage of the make-ahead tip below to cut down on last-minute preparations.

Prep: 20 minutes   Bake: 35 minutes   Stand: 5 minutes

1 6-ounce package long grain and wild rice mix	¾ cup chopped onion
1 4-ounce can sliced mushrooms, drained	1 tablespoon butter or margarine
2½ cups water	2 teaspoons prepared mustard
1 10-ounce package frozen chopped spinach	¼ teaspoon ground nutmeg
	1 8-ounce package cream cheese, cut into cubes*

1. In a 2-quart casserole combine rice mix and seasoning packet with mushrooms. In a medium saucepan combine the water, spinach, onion, butter, mustard and nutmeg. Bring to boiling; remove from heat. Stir spinach mixture; pour over rice mixture. Stir in cream cheese.

2. Bake, covered, in a 375° oven for 20 minutes. Stir mixture. Cover; bake 15 to 20 minutes more or until rice is tender. Stir again. Let stand 5 minutes before serving. **Makes 6 to 8 servings.**

*Note: This rice dish tastes just as creamy when you make it with reduced-fat cream cheese (Neufchâtel).

To make ahead: The casserole can be assembled ahead and refrigerated for up to 2 hours before baking. Add a few extra minutes to the baking time to heat the casserole through.

Cottage Cheese-Chive Biscuits,
page 71

Breads

Breads come in many shapes
and flavors in this treat-filled
chapter. Find cinnamon
rolls, a classic coffee cake,
chocolatey scones and other
ways to savor and share
some old-fashioned,
bakery-fresh goodness.

Cheddar Batter Bread

Never mind kneading and punching down. This loaf has all the home-baked goodness of a tricky yeast bread—but with none of the trickiness.

Prep: 15 minutes Rise: 20 minutes Bake: 40 minutes

1	tablespoon cornmeal	2	tablespoons butter
2	cups all-purpose flour	½	teaspoon salt
1	package fast-rising active	1	egg
	dry yeast	¾	cup shredded cheddar
¼	teaspoon onion powder		cheese (3 ounces)
¼	teaspoon black pepper	½	cup cornmeal
1	cup milk		
2	tablespoons sugar		

1. Grease the bottom and ½ inch up the sides of an 8×4×2-inch loaf pan. Sprinkle with the 1 tablespoon cornmeal; set aside. In a large mixing bowl stir together 1½ cups of the flour, the yeast, onion powder and pepper; set aside.

2. In a small saucepan combine milk, sugar, butter and salt. Stir together over medium heat just until mixture is warm (120°F to 130°F) and butter almost melts. Add milk mixture and egg to flour mixture. Beat with an electric mixer on low to medium speed for 30 seconds, scraping sides of bowl occasionally. Beat on high speed for 3 minutes. Stir in cheese and the ½ cup cornmeal. Stir in remaining flour. (The batter will be soft and sticky.) Spread batter evenly in prepared pan. Cover and let rise in a warm place until nearly double (about 20 minutes).

3. Bake, uncovered, in a 350° oven about 40 minutes or until bread sounds hollow when lightly tapped. If necessary, cover with foil during the last 15 minutes of baking to prevent overbrowning. Remove bread from pan. Cool on a wire rack. Serve warm.
Makes 1 loaf (16 servings).

Cottage Cheese-Chive Biscuits

Fresh home-baked bread on a weeknight? You bet! Drop biscuits are a breeze to make, so you can enjoy these anytime you crave them. Pictured on page 68.

Prep: 20 minutes   Bake: 15 minutes

2   cups all-purpose flour
2½   teaspoons baking powder
¼   teaspoon salt
6   tablespoons butter
¾   cup small-curd cottage
        cheese

⅔   cup milk
2   tablespoons snipped fresh
        chives or thinly sliced
        green onion tops

1. Line a baking sheet with foil; grease the foil. Set aside.

2. In a medium bowl combine flour, baking powder and salt. Using a pastry blender, cut in butter until mixture resembles coarse crumbs. Make a well in the center of flour mixture; set aside.

3. In a small bowl combine cottage cheese, milk and chives. Add cottage cheese mixture all at once to flour mixture. Using a fork, stir just until moistened.

4. Drop dough by generous tablespoonfuls onto prepared baking sheet. Bake in a 425° oven for 15 to 18 minutes or until golden. Remove from baking sheet; serve warm.
Makes 12 biscuits.

Tomato-Olive Spirals

Hot roll mix gives you a head start on these colorful, flavor-packed rolls. Serve alongside a selection of imported cheeses for an impressive appetizer spread.

Prep: 30 minutes   Rise: 30 minutes   Bake: 25 minutes

1 **16-ounce package hot roll mix**	1/4 **cup chopped green onions**
1/2 **cup oil-packed dried tomatoes**	1 **egg yolk, slightly beaten**
1 **8-ounce package cream cheese, softened**	1 **teaspoon cracked black pepper**
1 **3-ounce package cream cheese, softened**	1/2 **teaspoon dried oregano or thyme, crushed (optional)**
1/2 **cup finely chopped pitted ripe olives**	1 **slightly beaten egg**
	1 **tablespoon water**

1. Prepare the hot roll mix according to package directions. After kneading, divide the dough into thirds; cover and let rest for 5 minutes.

2. For filling, drain tomatoes, reserving oil. Chop tomatoes. Combine tomatoes, cream cheese, olives, green onions, egg yolk, pepper and, if desired, oregano. Stir in enough reserved tomato oil (about 1 tablespoon), if necessary, to make a filling that is easy to spread.

3. On a lightly floured surface, roll each portion of dough into a 14×11-inch rectangle. Spread one-third of the filling on top of each rectangle to within 1/2 inch of edges (filling amount will seem generous). Starting from long sides, roll up dough tightly. Pinch to seal seams. Place, seam side down, on a large greased baking sheet. Cover and let dough rise until nearly double (about 30 to 40 minutes).

4. Using a sharp knife, slash tops making three or four diagonal cuts about 1/4 inch deep. In a bowl combine the egg and water; brush onto rolls. Bake in a 375° oven 25 to 30 minutes or until golden. Carefully remove rolls from baking sheet and cool on a wire rack. Slice with a serrated knife into 1/2-inch slices. Serve warm or at room temperature. **Makes 3 loaves (72 spirals).**

To make ahead: Prepare and bake bread as directed; cool completely. Wrap loaves individually in heavy foil; freeze up to 3 months. To reheat, bake each wrapped loaf in a 300° oven 30 minutes or until heated through.

Applesauce-Rhubarb Muffins

Apples and rhubarb are a match made in heaven, as you'll see in these sweet, brown sugar-infused muffins.

Prep: 20 minutes Bake: 18 minutes

2 cups all-purpose flour	1⅓ cups packed brown sugar
1 cup whole wheat flour	1⅓ cups applesauce
2 teaspoons baking powder	½ cup cooking oil
2 teaspoons ground cinnamon	1½ cups chopped rhubarb
½ teaspoon baking soda	Crumbled sugar cubes or
½ teaspoon salt	cinnamon-sugar
2 eggs, beaten	

1. Lightly grease twenty-four 2½-inch muffin cups or line with paper baking cups.

2. In a large bowl combine all-purpose flour, whole wheat flour, baking powder, cinnamon, baking soda and salt. Make a well in the center; set aside.

3. In a medium bowl combine eggs, brown sugar, applesauce and cooking oil. Add egg mixture all at once to flour mixture. Stir just until moistened (batter should be lumpy). Fold in the rhubarb.

4. Spoon batter into prepared muffin cups, filling each two-thirds full. Sprinkle with crumbled sugar cubes. Bake in a 400° oven for 18 to 20 minutes or until a wooden toothpick inserted in center comes out clean. Cool in muffin cups on a wire rack for 5 minutes. Remove from muffin cups; serve warm. **Makes 24 muffins.**

Creamy Cinnamon Rolls

When you yearn for old-fashioned cinnamon rolls warm from the oven, make your wish come true in almost no time with this easy recipe. It starts with frozen sweet bread dough.

Prep: 20 minutes Rise: 1 hour Bake: 25 minutes

1   16-ounce loaf frozen sweet
      bread dough, thawed
2   tablespoons butter or
      margarine, melted
⅔   cup packed brown sugar

½   cup chopped walnuts
1   teaspoon ground cinnamon
½   cup whipping cream
⅔   cup sifted powdered sugar
      Milk

1. Lightly grease two 8×1½-inch round baking pans; set aside. On a lightly floured surface roll dough into a 20×8-inch rectangle. Brush with melted butter. In a small bowl combine brown sugar, nuts and cinnamon; sprinkle evenly over dough. Starting from a long side, roll up dough. Moisten edges and seal. Cut into 20 slices. Place slices, cut sides down, in prepared pans. Cover and let rise in a warm place until nearly double (1 to 1½ hours).

2. Slowly pour whipping cream over rolls. Bake in a 350° oven about 25 minutes or until golden brown. Let stand 1 minute. Loosen edges; invert onto serving plates. Scrape any caramel mixture left in pan onto rolls.

3. In a small bowl combine powdered sugar and enough milk (2 to 3 teaspoons) to make a glaze of drizzling consistency. Drizzle glaze over warm rolls. **Makes 20 rolls.**

Chocolate-Coconut Scones

For variety, try the fruit-studded version of these sweet treats.

Prep: 20 minutes Bake: 20 minutes

2 cups all-purpose flour	½ cup purchased unsweetened coconut milk or milk
3 tablespoons granulated sugar	⅓ cup shredded coconut
2 teaspoons baking powder	⅓ cup miniature semisweet chocolate pieces
¼ teaspoon salt	Milk (optional)
6 tablespoons butter	Coarse sugar (optional)
1 egg, beaten	

1. Lightly grease a baking sheet; set aside. In a medium bowl combine flour, the 3 tablespoons granulated sugar, the baking powder and salt. Using a pastry blender, cut in butter until mixture resembles coarse crumbs. Make a well in the center of flour mixture; set aside.

2. In a small bowl combine egg, coconut milk, coconut and chocolate pieces. Add egg mixture all at once to flour mixture. Using a fork, stir just until moistened.

3. Turn dough out onto a lightly floured surface. Quickly knead by folding and gently pressing dough for 10 to 12 strokes or until dough is nearly smooth. On the prepared baking sheet, pat or lightly roll dough into a 7-inch circle. Cut into 8 wedges; do not separate wedges. If desired, brush tops of scones with milk and sprinkle with coarse sugar.

4. Bake in a 400° oven for 20 to 25 minutes or until golden. Transfer to a wire rack; cool 5 minutes. Separate scones. Serve warm. **Makes 8 scones.**

To make ahead: Cool scones completely. Transfer to an airtight container or bag and store at room temperature for up to 3 days or in the freezer for up to 3 months.

Fruit Scones: Prepare scones as directed above except use milk instead of coconut milk, omit the coconut and substitute ½ cup dried blueberries or currants or snipped dried cherries, cranberries or raisins for the chocolate pieces.

Cream Cheese-Raspberry Coffee Cake

Forget doughnuts! When was the last time someone treated your office to a rich, made from-scratch coffee cake? Bring this treat for a change—it will brighten everyone's day.

Prep: 15 minutes   Bake: 30 minutes   Cool: 30 minutes

1   8-ounce package cream cheese or reduced-fat cream cheese (Neufchâtel), softened*
1   cup granulated sugar
½   cup butter, softened
1¾   cups all-purpose flour
2   eggs

¼   cup milk
½   teaspoon vanilla
1   teaspoon baking powder
½   teaspoon baking soda
¼   teaspoon salt
½   cup seedless raspberry preserves**
    Powdered sugar

1. Grease and flour a 13×9×2-inch baking pan; set aside.

2. In a large mixing bowl beat cream cheese, granulated sugar and butter with an electric mixer on medium speed until fluffy. Add half of the flour, the eggs, milk, vanilla, baking powder, baking soda and salt. Beat about 2 minutes or until well mixed. Beat in remaining flour on low speed until well mixed. Spread batter evenly in prepared baking pan. Spoon preserves in 8 to 10 portions on top of batter. With a knife, swirl preserves into batter to marble.

3. Bake in a 350° oven for 30 to 35 minutes or until a wooden toothpick, inserted near center, comes out clean. Cool slightly in pan on a wire rack. Sift powdered sugar over top. Cut into squares; serve warm. **Makes 24 servings.**

***Note:** Do not substitute fat-free cream cheese.

****Note:** If you wish, substitute your favorite flavor of preserves—such as strawberry or apricot—for the raspberry preserves.

Poppy Seed Tea Bread

Perfect for gift-giving, this quick bread is so tender and rich that it's almost like eating cake. Pictured on the back cover.

Prep: 15 minutes Bake: 50 minutes Cool: 10 minutes

3	cups all-purpose flour		1	cup cooking oil
2½	cups sugar		2	tablespoons poppy seeds
1½	teaspoons salt		1½	teaspoons vanilla
1½	teaspoons baking powder		1½	teaspoons almond extract
3	eggs, slightly beaten		1½	teaspoons butter flavoring
1½	cups milk			

1. Grease the bottom and ½ inch up sides of four 4½×2½×1½-inch loaf pans or two 8×4×2-inch loaf pans; set aside. In an extra-large bowl stir together flour, sugar, salt and baking powder. Make a well in the center of flour mixture; set aside.

2. In a medium bowl combine eggs, milk, cooking oil, poppy seeds, vanilla, almond extract and butter flavoring. Add egg mixture all at once to flour mixture. Stir just until moistened.

3. Spoon batter into the prepared pans. Bake in a 325° oven for 50 to 55 minutes for the 4½-inch loaf pans or 60 to 70 minutes for the 8-inch loaf pans or until a toothpick inserted near the center comes out clean. Cool in pans on a wire rack for 10 minutes. Remove loaves from pans. Cool completely on wire rack. Wrap and store overnight before slicing. **Makes four 4½-inch loaves or two 8-inch loaves (32 servings).**

Chocolate Mousse Torte, page 88

Sweets

*The sweet shop is open, so
come on in! Whether you need
a spectacular finish to a
glamorous dinner party,
creative candies for gift-giving
or a yummy cookie for an
after-school treat, this is
where you'll find it.*

WISCONSIN *A Salute to the Great Mid*
Flavors From Your Hometown
MICHIGA
MIN
SOU
ILL
NEB

Buttery Cashew Brittle

Peanut brittle is a best-loved holiday recipe. Now make the treat especially memorable with buttery cashews. You can also make the candy with almonds or macadamia nuts.

Prep: 15 minutes Cook: 45 minutes

2   cups sugar
1   cup light-colored corn syrup
½   cup water
1   cup butter

3   cups (about 12 ounces) raw cashews
1   teaspoon baking soda, sifted

1. Butter 2 baking sheets; set aside. In a 3-quart saucepan combine sugar, corn syrup and water. Cook and stir until sugar dissolves. Bring mixture to boiling; add butter and stir until butter is melted. Clip a candy thermometer to side of pan. Reduce heat to medium-low; continue boiling at a moderate, steady rate, stirring occasionally, until thermometer registers 280°F, soft-crack stage (about 35 minutes).

2. Stir in cashews; continue cooking over medium-low heat, stirring frequently, until the thermometer registers 300°F, hard-crack stage (10 to 15 minutes more).

3. Remove pan from heat; remove thermometer. Immediately stir in the baking soda, stirring constantly. Pour mixture onto prepared sheets.

4. As the cashew brittle cools, stretch it out by lifting and pulling from the edges with 2 forks. Loosen from pans as soon as possible; pick up sections and break them into bite-size pieces. Store tightly covered. **Makes about 2½ pounds.**

Three-in-One Cookies

What do you get when three popular drop cookie recipes—oatmeal, peanut butter and chocolate chip—get stirred into one? Delectable results, indeed!

Prep: 20 minutes Bake: 8 minutes per batch

¾ cup butter, softened	3 eggs
¾ cup peanut butter	1½ teaspoons vanilla
1¼ cups granulated sugar	2¼ cups all-purpose flour
1¼ cups packed brown sugar	2⅔ cups rolled oats
1½ teaspoons baking powder	1 10-ounce package miniature
½ teaspoon baking soda	milk chocolate kisses

1. In a large mixing bowl beat butter and peanut butter with an electric mixer on medium to high speed for 30 seconds. Add granulated sugar, brown sugar, baking powder and baking soda; beat until combined, scraping sides of bowl occasionally. Beat in eggs and vanilla until combined. Beat in flour. Stir in rolled oats with a wooden spoon. Stir in chocolate kisses.

2. Drop dough by rounded tablespoons 3 inches apart onto an ungreased cookie sheet. Slightly flatten dough with your hand, if desired. Bake in a 375° oven about 8 to 10 minutes or until edges are lightly brown. Transfer to wire racks; cool. Store in an airtight container at room temperature for up to 3 days. **Makes 60 to 72 cookies.**

To make ahead: Cool cookies completely. Place cookies in layers separated by waxed paper in an airtight container; cover. Store in the freezer up to 1 month.

Triple-Chocolate Coffee Brownies

You'll wonder what's more amazing: the deep rich flavor from the triple hit of chocolate or the fact that it all starts so simply from a mix!

Prep: 15 minutes Bake: 30 minutes

¼ cup water
2 teaspoons instant espresso coffee powder or 1 tablespoon instant coffee crystals
1 egg, beaten
1 19- to 21½-ounce package fudge brownie mix

¼ cup cooking oil
¼ cup coffee liqueur or water
¾ cup milk chocolate pieces
¾ cup white baking pieces
½ cup semisweet chocolate pieces
½ cup chopped walnuts or pecans

1. In a large bowl combine water and espresso powder; stir until dissolved. Stir in egg, brownie mix, oil, liqueur, milk chocolate pieces, white baking pieces, semisweet chocolate pieces and nuts. Stir just until combined. Spread batter into a greased 13×9×2-inch baking pan.

2. Bake in a 350° oven for 30 minutes. Cool brownies completely in pan on a wire rack. Cut into bars. **Makes 36 bars.**

Sesame-Apricot Thumbprints

These gems have the buttery richness of a shortbread cookie, but the apricot-sesame angle makes them a one-of-a-kind treat. Try them on a Christmas cookie tray—or any time of the year.

Prep: 45 minutes   Bake: 10 minutes per batch

1 cup butter, softened	$\frac{1}{3}$ cup sesame seeds
$\frac{1}{4}$ cup packed brown sugar	$\frac{1}{3}$ cup apricot preserves,
1 teaspoon almond extract	currant jelly and/or
$\frac{1}{4}$ teaspoon salt	grape jelly
2 cups all-purpose flour	

1. In a large mixing bowl beat butter with an electric mixer on medium to high speed for 30 seconds. Beat in brown sugar, almond extract and salt until light and fluffy. Beat in as much of the flour as you can with the mixer. Stir in any remaining flour. Shape dough into 1-inch balls; roll in sesame seeds.

2. Place balls 1½ inches apart on cookie sheets. Flatten balls slightly and indent centers with thumb or back of a spoon; fill with preserves and/or jelly, using about ½ teaspoon for each. Bake in a 375° oven about 10 to 12 minutes or until bottoms are lightly brown. Transfer to wire racks and cool. **Makes about 3 dozen cookies.**

Chocolate Mousse Torte

Shortcut artists take note! No one will ever know that this elegant dessert starts with a chocolate cake mix—the creamy mousse and chocolate topping make all the difference. Pictured on page 80.

Prep: 25 minutes Chill: 4 hours

1   package 1-layer-size devil's
     food cake mix
⅓ cup chocolate ice cream
     topping
4   ounces semisweet chocolate
2   tablespoons powdered sugar
2   tablespoons coffee liqueur
     or strong brewed coffee

2   egg yolks
½ cup whipping cream
1   tablespoon chocolate ice
     cream topping
     Fresh raspberries (optional)
     Mint leaves (optional)

1. Prepare and bake cake mix according to package directions, using a 9×1½-inch round baking pan. Cool in pan on a wire rack for 10 minutes. Remove cake from pan; cool completely. Place cake on a serving platter. Spread top with the ⅓ cup chocolate ice cream topping. Chill until needed.

2. For mousse, melt semisweet chocolate in a small saucepan over low heat, stirring often. Stir in powdered sugar, coffee liqueur and egg yolks. Cook and stir over medium heat about 3 minutes or until an instant-read thermometer registers 160°F. Remove from heat. Cool 10 minutes.

3. Place whipping cream in a small mixing bowl. Beat whipping cream with an electric mixer on medium speed just until soft peaks form. Stir half of the chocolate mixture into the whipped cream until combined. Fold in remaining chocolate mixture. Cover and chill for 5 to 10 minutes or until mixture just mounds. Spread onto cake top to within 1 inch of edge. Cover and chill for 4 to 6 hours.

4. To serve, drizzle cake with the 1 tablespoon chocolate ice cream topping. If desired, garnish with fresh raspberries and mint leaves. **Makes 10 servings.**

Apricot-Almond Crunch Pie

Prep: 35 minutes   Bake: 45 minutes

Pastry for Single-Crust Pie
(below)
Crumb Topping (below)
¾ cup granulated sugar
⅓ cup all-purpose flour

4 cups sliced, pitted apricots
(about 1¾ pounds),
peeled, if desired, or
4 cups frozen
unsweetened sliced
peaches
½ teaspoon almond extract

1. Prepare and roll out pastry. Line a 9-inch pie plate with the pastry. Trim and crimp edge as desired. Prepare Crumb Topping; set aside.

2. In a large bowl combine granulated sugar and flour. Add apricots or frozen peaches and almond extract. Gently toss until coated. (If using frozen peaches, let mixture stand for 45 minutes or until fruit is partially thawed but still icy.)

3. Transfer apricot or peach mixture to pastry-lined pie plate. Sprinkle Crumb Topping over filling.

4. Cover edge of the pie with foil. Fold a 12-inch square of foil into quarters. Cut a 7-inch hole out of the center. Unfold and loosely mold the foil over the pie's edge. Bake in a 375° oven for 25 minutes for fresh fruit (50 minutes for frozen fruit). Remove foil. Bake for 20 to 25 minutes more for fresh fruit (20 to 25 minutes for frozen fruit) or

until top is golden. Cool on a wire rack. **Makes 8 servings.**

Pastry for Single-Crust Pie: In a medium bowl stir together 1¼ cups flour and ¼ teaspoon salt. Using a pastry blender, cut in ⅓ cup shortening until pieces are pea size. Sprinkle 1 tablespoon cold water over part of the mixture, gently tossing with a fork. Push moistened dough to the side of the bowl. Repeat moistening dough, using 1 tablespoon of the water at a time, until all of the dough is moistened (about 4 to 5 tablespoons water). Form dough into a ball.

Crumb Topping: Stir together ½ cup all-purpose flour and ½ cup packed brown sugar. Using a pastry blender, cut in 3 tablespoons cold butter until mixture resembles coarse crumbs. Stir in ¼ cup slivered almonds.

Italian Cream Tarts

Prep: 45 minutes Bake: 17 minutes Stand: 20 minutes Chill: 3 hours

2	tablespoons sugar		1	17.3-ounce package frozen puff pastry (2 sheets)
1	tablespoon all-purpose flour Dash salt		½	cup mascarpone cheese
½	cup half-and-half or light cream		2	ounces semisweet chocolate, coarsely chopped
1	egg yolk, beaten		1½	teaspoons shortening Assorted fresh berries
4	teaspoons Grand Marnier or amaretto liqueur			

1. For the pastry cream, in a heavy small saucepan combine sugar, flour and salt; gradually stir in half-and-half. Cook and stir over medium heat until thickened and bubbly. Cook and stir for 1 minute more. In a medium bowl gradually stir about half of the hot mixture into the beaten egg yolk. Return all of the egg yolk mixture to the saucepan. Bring to a gentle boil; reduce heat. Cook and stir for 2 minutes. Remove from heat; transfer to a small bowl. Stir in liqueur. Cover surface with plastic wrap. Chill at least 2 hours. (Do not stir.)

2. Thaw pastry according to package directions. Unfold pastry sheets on a cutting surface. Using a 2½-inch cookie cutter, cut out 24 to 28 pastry rounds; place half on an ungreased baking sheet; prick each a few times with a fork. Using a 1½-inch cutter, cut the middle out of the remaining pastry rounds, reserving cutouts.

3. Brush the top edges of pastry rounds on baking sheet with water; top with rounds (with middles cut out). Press gently. Arrange small cutouts on another ungreased baking sheet, pricking each a few times with a fork. Bake in a 400° oven until puffed and golden, 10 to 12 minutes for tarts and 7 to 9 minutes for small cutouts. Cool completely.

4. Up to 1 hour before serving time, combine chilled pastry cream and mascarpone; stir until combined. Carefully spoon about 1 tablespoon of pastry cream into each tart shell. In a small saucepan melt semisweet chocolate and shortening together over low heat, stirring constantly. Remove from heat. Spread a thin layer of chocolate over tops of small cutouts. Drizzle remaining chocolate over the cream-filled tarts; refrigerate both until chocolate is set. To serve, arrange filled tarts and glazed cutouts around berries. Makes 12 to 14 servings.

Raspberry-Citrus Bars

These citrus bars get a little something extra with a sprinkling of fresh raspberries. Serve with a scoop of ice cream and call it dessert. Of course, they make a pretty special snack all on their own too.

Prep: 20 minutes Bake: 50 minutes

1	cup butter, softened
¾	cup sifted powdered sugar
2	cups all-purpose flour
4	eggs
1½	cups granulated sugar
⅓	cup orange juice

1	tablespoon finely shredded lemon peel
¼	cup all-purpose flour
1	teaspoon baking powder
1½	cups fresh raspberries and/or blueberries
	Powdered sugar

1. In a large mixing bowl beat butter with an electric mixer on medium speed for 30 seconds. Add the ¾ cup powdered sugar; beat until combined, scraping sides of the bowl occasionally. Add the 2 cups flour; beat until combined. Press mixture into the bottom of a greased 13×9×2-inch baking pan. Bake in a 350° oven for 20 minutes or until golden.

2. Meanwhile, for filling, in another large mixing bowl combine eggs, granulated sugar, orange juice, lemon peel, the ¼ cup flour and the baking powder. Beat with an electric mixer for 2 minutes or until combined. Sprinkle berries over crust. Pour filling over berries, arranging berries evenly with a spoon.

3. Bake for 30 to 35 minutes or until light brown and filling is set. Cool in pan on a wire rack. Cut into bars. Just before serving, sprinkle with powdered sugar. **Makes 32 bars.**

To make ahead: Cover and store in the refrigerator up to 2 days. Or place cut bars in a storage container or freezer bag and freeze up to 1 month. Thaw, covered, in the refrigerator.

Strawberry Cloud Nine

This dessert calls for reduced-fat products, but if you feel like splurging, go ahead and use whole-fat cream cheese, sour cream and dessert topping.

Prep: 15 minutes Bake: 1 hour 20 minutes Stand: 30 minutes Chill: 1 hour

Meringue Shells (below)
¾ **of an 8-ounce package (6 ounces) reduced-fat cream cheese (Neufchâtel), softened**
½ **cup light dairy sour cream**
2 **tablespoons sugar**
½ **teaspoon vanilla**
¼ **of an 8-ounce container frozen light dessert whipped topping, thawed**
1 **ounce semisweet chocolate, cut up**
½ **teaspoon shortening**
3 **cups hulled small fresh strawberries**
¼ **cup strawberry jelly**

1. Prepare and bake Meringue Shells. In a medium bowl beat together cream cheese, sour cream, sugar and vanilla with an electric mixer on medium speed until smooth. Gently stir in thawed topping. Spread evenly in Meringue Shells. Cover and chill about 1 hour.

2. In a heavy small saucepan melt semisweet chocolate with shortening over low heat; cool. Drizzle over tops and sides of filled shells. Arrange berries, hulled end down, on top of cream cheese filling. In a small saucepan heat jelly over low heat just until melted. Add 1 to 2 teaspoons water to thin. Drizzle over berries. **Makes 8 servings.**

Meringue Shells: Let 3 egg whites stand in a large mixing bowl at room temperature for 30 minutes. Meanwhile, cover a baking sheet with parchment paper or foil; draw eight 3-inch circles on paper or foil. Add ½ teaspoon vanilla and ¼ teaspoon cream of tartar to egg whites. Beat with an electric mixer on medium speed until soft peaks form (tips curl). Add 1 cup sugar, a tablespoon at a time, beating on high speed until very stiff peaks form (tips stand straight) and sugar is almost dissolved. Using a pastry bag, pipe the meringue onto the circles on the paper, building up the sides to form shells. (Or use the back of a spoon to spread the meringue over the circles, building up the sides.) Bake in a 300° oven for 20 minutes. Turn oven off; let meringues dry in oven with door closed at least 1 hour (do not open door). Peel off paper. Store in an airtight container.

Coffee Cheesecake

Looking for a surefire finale for your next dinner party? There's something about a silky cheesecake that never fails to impress. Add a nutty, chocolate crust and a touch of coffee in the filling, and it's a dynamite dessert indeed.

Prep: 20 minutes Bake: 45 minutes Cool: 1¾ hours Chill: 4 hours

½ cup graham cracker crumbs
½ cup chocolate cookie
    crumbs
½ cup ground hazelnuts or
    almonds
3 tablespoons sugar
¼ cup butter, melted

3 8-ounce packages cream
   cheese, softened
1 cup sugar
3 tablespoons all-purpose flour
1 teaspoon vanilla
3 eggs, slightly beaten
¼ cup coffee liqueur or cooled
   espresso coffee

1. Generously grease the bottom and sides of an 8-inch springform pan; set aside. For crust, in a bowl combine cracker crumbs, cookie crumbs, nuts and the 3 tablespoons sugar. Stir in melted butter. Press crumb mixture firmly onto bottom and 2 inches up the side of prepared pan. Set aside.

2. For filling, in a large bowl beat cream cheese, the 1 cup sugar, the flour and vanilla with an electric mixer on medium to high speed until fluffy, scraping sides of bowl as necessary. Stir in eggs and liqueur until just combined. Pour filling into crust-lined pan.

3. Place in a shallow baking pan in the oven. Bake in a 375° oven for 45 to 50 minutes or until center appears nearly set when gently shaken.

4. Cool in springform pan on wire rack for 15 minutes. Loosen sides of cake from pan and cool 30 minutes more. Remove sides from pan; cool 1 hour. Cover and chill in the refrigerator at least 4 hours or up to 24 hours before serving. **Makes 16 servings.**